DECISION MAKING
Discerning the Will of God

JUNE HUNT

AspirePress

Torrance, California

Decision Making: Discerning the Will of God
Copyright © 2013 Hope For The Heart
All rights reserved.
Aspire Press, a division of Rose Publishing, Inc.
4733 Torrance Blvd., #259
Torrance, California 90503 USA
www.aspirepress.com

Register your book at www.aspirepress.com/register
Get inspiration via email, sign up at www.aspirepress.com

Printed in the United States of America
020813DP

CONTENTS

ear friend,

Recently I've been thinking about my own decision making—specifically, what has caused me to make the inexcusable decisions that later I would come to regret. I wish I could blame these wrong decisions on ignorance or indigestion or a "bad hair day!" However, in good conscience, I cannot justify such blame-shifting! The truthful answer is this: I prioritized "passion over principle."

Sometimes, if I want to better understand myself or others, I look back at the past for a clue or two. One day, I peered back and asked myself, *When was the first time I willfully chose to do what I knew was wrong?* The answer was immediate: My "life of crime" began when I was quite young. Mother had gone into a drugstore to purchase some needed items for the house. As we walked down the aisle, she stopped to look at an item on the left. At the same time, I looked to the right, and there it was—a 3 MUSKETEERS® candy bar! I was now eye-level with *rows* of 3 MUSKETEERS® candy bars! (Mind you, this was not just *any* candy bar. This chocolate delicacy had long been advertised as "The biggest nickel candy bar"!)

It was at this very moment that I chose passion over principle. Yes, of course, I knew I should not steal. I knew that principle, yet somehow, one lone candy bar seemed to slip into my right hand (and it was *a perfect fit*). Quickly, through the big glass doors, I scurried outside, took a right, and then went around the corner—because I needed to get out of sight so as not to get caught red-handed ... or chocolate-handed! As fast as I could, I tore open the wrapper and literally crammed the candy bar into my mouth. I had to hurry to get rid of the evidence and get back inside the store as soon as possible.

With my heart pounding, I anxiously followed some big, tall people through the large glass doors leading back into the drugstore. Mother was at the counter completing her purchases. Within moments, we were headed for home. And all was well with the world. All was well—until Mother looked over at me and said, "Why do you have chocolate on your face?"

"Chocolate? What chocolate?" I rapidly replied.

Mother pulled the car over to get a closer look. Sure enough, all the evidence had *not* been eliminated. Several smudges of chocolate were much too visible.

Calmly, she continued, "June, where did you get the chocolate?"

I mumbled something, which amounted to nothing. After further questioning, I was forced to admit my thievery. (No other explanation would make sense.)

Then humiliation upon humiliation: Mother drove me back to the store not only to pay for the "stolen property," but also to confess my crime in front of the manager.

The surprised store manager asked what I had stolen. With downcast eyes—and a voice barely above a whisper—I eked out, "I don't remember." I just didn't want to admit my extravagance: I had stolen a 3 MUSKETEERS®—"The biggest nickel candy bar in existence"!

A moment later, Mother handed me the money to give to the manager. (She made *me* do it all—ugh!)

Obviously, that embarrassing scene—especially the way Mother handled it—made a strong impression on me because I remember it to this day, decades later.

Now, I know someone will say, "That's nothing! That's so insignificant. That's just a child's decision to steal a nickel candy bar from a store, and in no more than 30 minutes, everything was resolved."

The issue is not *what* I stole, *when* I stole, *where* I stole, or from *whom* I stole. The crux of the matter is *why* I stole. In simplest terms, I chose to yield to temptation. I chose passion over principle.

The aftermath of prioritizing passion can be devastating when wrong decisions result in a loss of respect, a loss of reputation, or a loss of a relationship.

That is the *why* of this small book: to help you make decisions that you will never regret—decisions that line up with the whole counsel of God, and decisions that are in the perfect will of God. Only then can you live a life of perfect peace.

Yours in the Lord's hope,

June

June Hunt

"My son, do not forget my teaching,
but keep my commands in your heart,
for they will prolong your life many years
and bring you peace and prosperity."
(Proverbs 3:1–2)

DECISION MAKING
Discerning the Will of God

"He loves me, he loves me not, he loves me, he loves me not." Through the ages, children have played this simple game of deciding whether someone loved them or not by plucking petals from a daisy one-by-one. The last petal supposedly reveals the answer—but what an unreliable way to make decisions! And just as unreliable is making choices based on changeable circumstances or the cries of a crowd. Wise decisions are made by discerning the will of God, and God delights in revealing His will to those willing to do His will. And His will is clearly revealed in His Word.

"Do not merely listen to the word,
and so deceive yourselves.
Do what it says."
(James 1:22)

DEFINITIONS

We make decisions every day. Many are of little significance; a few will change our lives forever. Do you make quick decisions by "doing what comes naturally," or do you struggle with delay because of a paralysis of analysis? Many bad choices are made in life because we do not take the time to discover God's perfect will for our lives. Be assured, God doesn't play "hide-and-seek" as you try to discover His will. The more intimately you draw close to the heart of God, the more clearly you will know the will of God. And as you sincerely begin to place His desires above your own desires, He will be faithful to point the way. Let this be the prayer of your heart:

> "I desire to do your will, my God;
> your law is within my heart."
> (Psalm 40:8)

Making a decision is a process that includes making a choice or judgment about an attitude or action. Decisions are an act of the will, and they are always influenced by either the mind or the emotions.

▶ The Old Testament Hebrew word *abah*, which means "to breathe after" or "to be acquiescent," is used to indicate a willingness to accept or comply.[1]

- **Your decisions receive God's blessing when you are willing to obey God.**

  "If you are willing and obedient, you will eat the good things of the land" (Isaiah 1:19).

▶ The Greek word *krino* is one of the many New Testament words that can be translated "to decide." This Greek word means "to distinguish, to decide mentally, to determine or resolve."[2]

- **Your decisions should be based on what you know to be God's revealed will.**

  "As for the Gentile believers, we have written to them our decision that they should abstain from food sacrificed to idols, from blood, from the meat of strangled animals and from sexual immorality" (Acts 21:25).

▶ Another Old Testament Hebrew word, *bachar*, which means "to select," is also translated "to prefer or desire."[3]

- **Your decisions reveal the desires of your heart.**

    "I have chosen the way of faithfulness; I have set my heart on your laws." (Psalm 119:30)

- **Your decisions are ultimately determined by what you desire the most. The fundamental principle for each of us becomes, "Do I choose to please myself, or do I choose to please the Lord?"**

    "But if serving the LORD seems undesirable to you, then choose for yourselves this day whom you will serve ... But as for me and my household, we will serve the LORD" (Joshua 24:15).

WHAT IS the Meaning of "Will"?

Like a prism, the word *will* reflects many different sides.[4]

▶ When making a choice, you are communicating your will.

▶ The word *will* is also used to express the desire or mandate of someone having authority. (God reveals His will.)

▶ Another meaning of the word *will* carries the idea of having a disposition to act according to one's desired goals. (A child may be born with a strong will.)

▶ Further, by use of your own will, you can exercise power and control over your own actions or emotions.

"Father, if you are willing, take this cup from me; yet not my will, but yours be done."
(Luke 22:42)

QUESTION: "What did Jesus mean in Matthew 6:10 when He prayed to the heavenly Father, 'Your will be done, on earth as it is in heaven'?"

ANSWER: Jesus modeled a heart of submission to the will of His Father because He knew God's will would ultimately be best. The meanings of the following Greek words used in the New Testament describe why **God's will** should always be preferred.[5]

▶ *Thelema* means "a determination, choice or a desire of the heart."

  ▪ God's will is His heart's desire for you.

▶ *Boulema* means "a plan of the mind; a deliberate design and purpose."

  ▪ God's will is His ultimate plan and purpose for you.

▶ *Eudokia* means "good and pleasing."

  ▪ God's will is ultimately pleasing and good for you.

"Your kingdom come, your will be done, on earth as it is in heaven."
(Matthew 6:10)

WHAT IS Meant When Scripture Refers to the Will of God?

Scripture refers to a three-dimensional picture of the "will of God"—***perfect, permissive,*** and ***prevailing***.

1 God's Perfect Will

"Do not conform to the pattern of this world, but be transformed by the renewing of your mind. Then you will be able to test and approve what God's will is—his good, pleasing and perfect will" (Romans 12:2).

- God has an ideal plan.
- God's plan is pleasing and good.

Example:

God's perfect will is for everyone to repent of sin and for no one to perish.

"The Lord ... is patient with you, not wanting anyone to perish, but everyone to come to repentance" (2 Peter 3:9).

2 God's Permissive Will

"They hated knowledge and did not choose to fear the LORD" (Proverbs 1:29).

- God permits each person to exercise free will in opposition to His will.
- God is ultimately sovereign over all that He permits.

Example:

God's permissive will allows everyone the option of choosing right or wrong, spiritual life or spiritual death, being blessed or being cursed.

"This day I call the heavens and the earth as witnesses against you that I have set before you life and death, blessings and curses. Now choose life, so that you and your children may live" (Deuteronomy 30:19).

3 God's Prevailing Will

"Many are the plans in a person's heart, but it is the LORD's purpose that prevails" (Proverbs 19:21).

- God's plans cannot be thwarted.
- God's ultimate purposes are achieved because He is sovereign.

Example:

God's prevailing will is to grant full forgiveness and a home in heaven to all who repent of their sins and trust in Jesus Christ as their Lord and Savior.

"I know that you can do all things; no purpose of yours can be thwarted" (Job 42:2).

QUESTION: "Has God already determined His will for me?"

ANSWER: Yes. God's will for you was prepared in advance.

> "For we are God's handiwork, created in Christ Jesus to do good works, which God prepared in advance for us to do."
> (Ephesians 2:10)

QUESTION: "Can I actually know God's will for my life?"

ANSWER: Yes. God desires to reveal His will to you in a personal way.

> "The God of our ancestors has chosen you to know his will and to see the Righteous One and to hear words from his mouth."
> (Acts 22:14)

QUESTION: "How does God reveal His will?"

ANSWER: God reveals His will primarily through ...

▶ **The Spirit of God**

> " ... when he, the Spirit of truth, comes, he will guide you into all the truth. He will not speak on his own; he will speak only what he hears, and he will tell you what is yet to come" (John 16:13).

▶ The Word of God

"Your word is a lamp for my feet, a light on my path" (Psalm 119:105).

QUESTION: "Will God reveal the whole blueprint of my life?"

ANSWER: Only God sees the whole picture—the past, present, and future of your life. Discovering God's will is like reading a scroll. He teaches and counsels you as He unrolls the scroll one day at a time.

"I will instruct you and teach you in the way you should go; I will counsel you with my loving eye on you." (Psalm 32:8)

QUESTION: "What if God's will seems undesirable?"

ANSWER: God's will may seem undesirable and unpleasant when your heart is following your own desires and not trusting God.

"Take delight in the LORD, and he will give you the desires of your heart." (Psalm 37:4)

QUESTION: "Why does God's will for me sometimes include sorrow and affliction?"

ANSWER: Suffering allows you to see God's sufficiency as you learn to depend on Him.

"It was good for me to be afflicted so that I might learn your decrees." (Psalm 119:71)

God blesses ...

▶ **Decisions** that He initiates

"I instruct you in the way of wisdom and lead you along straight paths" (Proverbs 4:11).

▶ **Decisions** that line up with His Word

"Direct my footsteps according to your word; let no sin rule over me" (Psalm 119:133).

▶ **Decisions** that accomplish His purpose

" ... it is God who works in you to will and to act in order to fulfill his good purpose" (Philippians 2:13).

▶ **Decisions** that depend on His strength

"I can do all this through him who gives me strength" (Philippians 4:13).

▶ **Decisions** that result in giving Him glory

" ... whether you eat or drink or whatever you do, do it all for the glory of God" (1 Corinthians 10:31).

▶ **Decisions** that promote justice, kindness, and humility

" ... what does the LORD require of you? To act justly and to love mercy and to walk humbly with your God" (Micah 6:8).

▶ **Decisions** that reflect His character

"Don't let anyone look down on you because you are young, but set an example for the believers in speech, in conduct, in love, in faith and in purity" (1 Timothy 4:12).

▶ **Decisions** that come from faith

" ... without faith it is impossible to please God, because anyone who comes to him must believe that he exists and that he rewards those who earnestly seek him" (Hebrews 11:6).

▶ **Decisions** that consider the interests of others

" ... not looking to your own interests but each of you to the interests of the others" (Philippians 2:4).

▶ **Decisions** that are bathed in prayer

" ... pray continually" (1 Thessalonians 5:17).

WHAT IS God's Heart on Decision Making?

God's heart on decision making is to *help us with our decisions.* God empathizes with our struggles; He is eager to lead us according to His infinite wisdom and perfect plan. None of us knows what the future holds. At times we truly don't know which way to turn, but when we seek our all-knowing God, He never fails to direct us down paths for our good and for His glory.

Consider what an indescribably awesome privilege it is that the God of the universe, the Creator of billions of galaxies and even more stars, cares about *your decisions* concerning your health, your job, your marriage, and your children. He longs to help you with all of your decisions. There is no need to fear that something is too small or insignificant to take to Him. If it matters to you, *it matters to Him.*

> "I lift up my eyes to the mountains—
> where does my help come from?
> My help comes from the LORD,
> the Maker of heaven and earth."
> (Psalm 121:1–2)

God's heart on decision making as it relates to *Him*:

▶ **EAGER:** He is eager to help us in our time of need.

"He reached down from on high and took hold of me; he drew me out of deep waters" (Psalm 18:16).

▶ **SYMPATHETIC:** He is sympathetic when we experience strenuous circumstances.

"Why, my soul, are you downcast? Why so disturbed within me? Put your hope in God, for I will yet praise him, my Savior and my God" (Psalm 43:5).

▶ **MOVED:** He is moved when we trust Him at all times.

"When Jesus heard this, he was amazed and said to those following him, 'Truly I tell you, I have not found anyone in Israel with such great faith'" (Matthew 8:10).

▶ **DETERMINED**: He is determined to use opportunities of uncertainty to deepen our fellowship with Him.

"When hard pressed, I cried to the LORD; he brought me into a spacious place" (Psalm 118:5).

▶ **ATTENTIVE**: He is attentive to direct the circumstances of our lives in accordance with His perfect plan.

"Teach me to do your will, for you are my God; may your good Spirit lead me on level ground" (Psalm 143:10).

▶ **WILLING**: He is willing to tap into His unlimited resources to wisely guide our lives.

"Counsel and sound judgment are mine; I have insight, I have power" (Proverbs 8:14).

▶ **FAITHFUL**: He is faithful to lead us all the days of our lives.

"Even to your old age and gray hairs I am he, I am he who will sustain you. I have made you and I will carry you ... " (Isaiah 46:4).

▶ **GENEROUS**: He is generous in granting wisdom to us if we ask for it in faith.

"If any of you lacks wisdom, you should ask God, who gives generously to all without finding fault,

and it will be given to you. But when you ask, you must believe and not doubt, because the one who doubts is like a wave of the sea, blown and tossed by the wind. That person should not expect to receive anything from the Lord" (James 1:5-7).

God's heart on decision making as it relates to *us*:

▶ **SINCERE**: He wants us to sincerely seek His will.

"And you, my son Solomon, acknowledge the God of your father, and serve him with wholehearted devotion and with a willing mind, for the LORD searches every heart and understands every desire and every thought. If you seek him, he will be found by you; but if you forsake him, he will reject you forever" (1 Chronicles 28:9).

▶ **DESIRE**: He wants us to desire His will above our own.

"Father, if you are willing, take this cup from me; yet not my will, but yours be done" (Luke 22:42).

▶ **PATIENCE**: He wants us to patiently wait for a word from Him.

"I wait for the LORD, my whole being waits, and in his word I put my hope" (Psalm 130:5).

▶ **LOOK**: He wants us to look to Him to speak to us through His Word.

"Accept instruction from his mouth and lay up his words in your heart" (Job 22:22).

▶ **APPROACH**: He wants us to approach him with an honest heart and a clear conscience.

"I know, my God, that you test the heart and are pleased with integrity. All these things I have given willingly and with honest intent" (1 Chronicles 29:17).

▶ **VALUE**: He wants us to value the counsel of His Word above the counsel of people.

"To God belong wisdom and power; counsel and understanding are his ... We are not trying to please people but God, who tests our hearts" (Job 12:13; 1 Thessalonians 2:4).

▶ **WAIT**: He wants us to wait until His Word and the prompting of His Spirit are in agreement.

"I will not venture to speak of anything except what Christ has accomplished through me in leading the Gentiles to obey God by what I have said and done—by the power of signs and wonders, through the power of the Spirit of God. So from Jerusalem all the way around to Illyricum, I have fully proclaimed the gospel of Christ" (Romans 15:18–19).

▶ **CONNECT**: He wants us to look to circumstances in connection with His Word, the Spirit's leading, and our peace of mind.

"When they came to the border of Mysia, they tried to enter Bithynia, but the Spirit of Jesus would not allow them to" (Acts 16:7).

CHARACTERISTICS OF MAKING GOOD DECISIONS

Gideon couldn't conceive of carrying out the gargantuan task the Lord was requiring of him. He was too insignificant, too weak, too ... whatever! How could Gideon—the least in his father's house and identified with the weakest clan in Manasseh—ever deliver Israel from such a monstrous enemy army?

Although God had directly spoken to him, this godly young man still felt insecure about making the right decision. To make sure he had actually heard from God, twice Gideon asked for a supernatural sign. The first night he put out a fleece and asked God to make it wet and the ground dry. The next night Gideon asked God to make the fleece dry and the ground wet. Although God honored both of Gideon's requests, today Christians have the indwelling Holy Spirit, who counsels them, and the *"word more fully confirmed"* (2 Peter 1:19 ESV). Therefore, we are not to look to supernatural events to reveal the will of God.

"Gideon said to God, 'If you will save Israel by my hand as you have promised—look, I will place a wool fleece on the threshing floor. If there is dew only on the fleece and all the ground is dry, then I

will know that you will save Israel by my hand, as you said.' And that is what happened. Gideon rose early the next day; he squeezed the fleece and wrung out the dew—a bowlful of water. Then Gideon said to God, 'Do not be angry with me. Let me make just one more request. Allow me one more test with the fleece, but this time make the fleece dry and let the ground be covered with dew.' That night God did so. Only the fleece was dry; all the ground was covered with dew" (Judges 6:36–40).

Some people will always want visible signs to discern God's will, yet these signs are based on normal occurrences such as chance phone calls or letters. If you insist on "putting out a fleece," make sure the sign is supernatural. Suggestion: On a hot summer day, why not ask for a snowstorm!

WHAT ARE Six Methods of Decision Making?

If you could, wouldn't you want to know the future? If you could see the outcome, wouldn't it make your decisions a lot more accurate? Today people seek guidance through a plethora of occult practices. They search for answers in newspaper columns, carnival booths, and psychic hotlines. Astrologers, palm readers, and fortune-tellers toting tarot cards all claim to speak for "God." But the God of the Bible says these dramatic ways are *"detestable"* (Deuteronomy 18:9). He warns us, *"Do not turn to mediums or seek out spiritists, for you will be defiled by them. I am the* LORD *your God"* (Leviticus 19:31).

"There is a way that appears to be right, but in the end it leads to death." (Proverbs 14:12)

Making decisions can be approached in various ways, but most will fall into one of the following six methods or a combination of some of them. Not all methods of decision making will prove to be profitable.

1 DRAMATIC METHOD

Some people misuse Scripture by flipping open the Bible and *pointing to some random Scripture for guidance* without considering the context. Others expect God to come through with a spectacular, supernatural sign that will give proof of His will in a given situation.

Yet, God says, *"the Advocate, the Holy Spirit, whom the Father will send in my name, will teach you all things ... "* (John 14:26).

2 DEFAULTING METHOD

Scripture tells us there is an appropriate time to delegate duties and to seek counsel, but ultimately we are responsible for our own choices. We can even be so *pressured by the opinions of others* that it becomes easier just to let others make decisions for us, even when we think they are wrong.

Yet, God says, *"He will be eating curds and honey when he knows enough to reject the wrong and choose the right"* (Isaiah 7:15).

3 DELAYING METHOD

Many people *choose to procrastinate* when a decision is due, hoping that "it will all come out well in the end." They allow circumstances to determine the outcome. However, not to decide is actually a decision. Their delay tactics are filled with superfluous activities that do not include placing a high priority on knowing God's will through prayer, biblical counsel, and intimacy with the Lord.

Yet, God says, *"Their hearts are always going astray, and they have not known my ways"* (Hebrews 3:10).

4 DEDUCTIVE METHOD

The Christian life is to be a life of balance between human deduction and spiritual insight. If we become solely *analytical in thinking* through a situation and choose to rely completely on logic, we will miss God's way.

Yet, God says, *"My thoughts are not your thoughts, neither are your ways my ways, declares the LORD"* (Isaiah 55:8).

5 DESIROUS METHOD

Too many people allow their emotions to have "soul control." This means allowing *feelings to determine their behavior.* God gave us emotions, but He never intended emotions to be our "decision makers." Many of us don't even realize that we often have an "if it feels good, it must be good" mentality.

Yet, God says, *"Those who trust in themselves are fools, but those who walk in wisdom are kept safe"* (Proverbs 28:26).

6 DISCERNING METHOD *(the best method)*

To be discerning is to *grasp what may not be evident*, that is, "to have insight and understanding by going beyond what seems obvious."[6] Spiritual discernment, therefore, is wisdom to determine what is true, appropriate, and superior in the eyes of God, regardless of how things may seem.

Yet, God says, *"The person without the Spirit does not accept the things that come from the Spirit of God but considers them foolishness, and cannot understand them because they are discerned only through the Spirit"* (1 Corinthians 2:14).

Biblical Example

Noah and the Ark (Genesis 6:5–22)

"Noah was a righteous man" who walked with God. Because of his personal relationship with the Lord, he knew God's voice and, having the heart of a servant, was willing to do *"all that God commanded"*—even though his construction of an ark (a mammoth structure on dry ground) made Noah look foolish in the eyes of his friends.

Without knowing the future, Noah focused on what God was doing and adjusted his life according to God's plan rather than asking God to bless his own plan. Logically, Noah could have chosen to build a place of worship. After all, weren't the people morally corrupt and spiritually bankrupt? Yes, they were, but God knew the people would remain unrepentant—something Noah did not know. If Noah had built a church, he and his family, along with the church, would have washed away.

> "Noah did everything [built the ark];
> just as God commanded him."
> (Genesis 6:22)

WHAT ARE Tests for Decision Making?

He was scared to death—but it was to the *dead* that Saul turned for guidance!

The enemy army had gathered for war against his smaller country. He wanted counsel from God, but *"He [Saul] inquired of the Lord, but the Lord did not answer him"* (1 Samuel 28:6). Desperate for supernatural insight, Saul disguised himself and went to a medium (a practice forbidden by God). He asked to talk with the beloved prophet Samuel, who had died. After Samuel appeared and after Saul complained that God no longer answered him, Samuel replied, *"Why do you consult me, now that the Lord has departed from you and become your enemy?"* (1 Samuel 28:16).

The Lord would not answer Saul because he had continually defied the commands of God—and since he did not reflect the heart of God, he became the enemy of God. When faced with a decision, we need to see whether we "pass the test" so that our decisions will be blessed.

Eight Tests of Decision Making

From God's perspective, decisions are not to be determined by random selection, supernatural events, people's opinions, delay tactics, analytical thinking, or good feelings. God wants you to measure your decisions by His standards. Rather than testing God, test yourself against the following eight Scriptures. This will help you to make choices that are pleasing to the Lord.

"Live as children of light ... and find out what pleases the Lord." (Ephesians 5:8, 10)

1. SCRIPTURAL TEST

"Has God already spoken about it in His Word?"

Example: Marrying a nonbeliever in hopes of drawing the spouse to Christ even though 2 Corinthians 6:14 says, *"Do not be yoked together with unbelievers."*

"All Scripture is God-breathed and is useful for teaching, rebuking, correcting and training in righteousness" (2 Timothy 3:16).

2. SECRECY TEST

"Would it bother me if everyone knew this was my choice?"

Example: Thinking no one is hurt by keeping an overpayment of returned cash or credit

"The integrity of the upright guides them, but the unfaithful are destroyed by their duplicity" (Proverbs 11:3).

3. SURVEY TEST

"What if everyone followed my example?"

Example: Assuming a little trash tossed out the car window will never be noticed on a busy highway

" ... set an example for the believers in speech, in conduct, in love, in faith and in purity" (1 Timothy 4:12).

4. SPIRIT TEST

"Am I being people-pressured or Spirit-led?"

Example: Accepting a commitment of time that has not been affirmed in your spirit by God

"Am I now trying to win the approval of human beings, or of God? Or am I trying to please people? If I were still trying to please people, I would not be a servant of Christ" (Galatians 1:10).

5. STUMBLING TEST

"Could this cause another person to stumble?"

Example: Having an alcoholic drink in a public place

"It is better not to eat meat or drink wine or to do anything else that will cause your brother or sister to fall" (Romans 14:21).

6. SERENITY TEST

"Have I prayed and received peace about this decision?"

Example: Deciding to make any major change without praying and waiting on God's peace for confirmation

"Do not be anxious about anything, but in every situation, by prayer and petition, with thanksgiving, present your requests to God. And the peace of God, which transcends all understanding, will guard your hearts and your minds in Christ Jesus" (Philippians 4:6–7).

7. SANCTIFICATION TEST

"Will this keep me from growing in the character of Christ?"

Example: Failing to obey God when He prompts you to do something that is difficult or burdensome

"... we all, who with unveiled faces contemplate the Lord's glory, are being transformed into his image with ever-increasing glory, which comes from the Lord, who is the Spirit" (2 Corinthians 3:18).

8. SUPREME TEST

"Does this glorify God?"

Example: Conforming to the standards of the world by living a lifestyle beyond my means

"So whether you eat or drink or whatever you do, do it all for the glory of God." (1 Corinthians 10:31)

CAUSES OF DIFFICULTY

He had it all—*except wisdom.*

Flocks by the thousands grazed in his fields, a beautiful wife adorned his arm, and food and drink were abundant in his household. But a foolish choice made by Nabal—whose name means "fool"—*would prove fatal.*

David and his small, young army had been protecting Nabal's shepherds and sheep. Then during a time of shearing and feasting, David asked Nabal for food to sustain his men in the wilderness. This reasonable request was met only with resentment and an insulting refusal. As a result of Nabal's selfish, self-absorbed, self-indulgent decision, he met his death prematurely. Ten days later, the Lord took his life.

Our decisions can be costly when they are made with mixed motives and spiritual immaturity.

"Who is this David? Who is this son of Jesse?" (1 Samuel 25:10), Nabal spouts condescendingly in contempt.

Who was David? Nabal likened him to a runaway slave, but this David, whom Nabal refused to help, was *the next king of Israel.*

Enraged by Nabal's response, David directs 400 of his men to arm themselves to take vengeance on Nabal and his household.

> **"David had just said, 'It's been useless— all my watching over this fellow's property in the wilderness so that nothing of his was missing. He has paid me back evil for good. May God deal with David, be it ever so severely, if by morning I leave alive one male of all who belong to him!'"**
> **(1 Samuel 25:21–22)**

Common reasons for having clouds of confusion engulfing your decision-making process include:

▶ **Not having pure motives**

"When you ask, you do not receive, because you ask with wrong motives, that you may spend what you get on your pleasures" (James 4:3).

▶ **Not surrendering your will**

"My Father, if it is possible, may this cup be taken from me. Yet not as I will, but as you will" (Matthew 26:39).

▶ Not seeking God's will through His Word

"Your word is a lamp for my feet, a light on my path" (Psalm 119:105).

▶ Not repenting of known sin in my life

"If I had cherished sin in my heart, the Lord would not have listened" (Psalm 66:18).

▶ Not praying continually and earnestly

"If any of you lacks wisdom, you should ask God, who gives generously to all without finding fault, and it will be given to you" (James 1:5).

▶ Not expecting God to answer

"But when you ask, you must believe and not doubt, because the one who doubts is like a wave of the sea, blown and tossed by the wind. That person should not expect to receive anything from the Lord" (James 1:6–7).

▶ Not patiently waiting for God's timing

"And so after waiting patiently, Abraham received what was promised" (Hebrews 6:15).

▶ Not willing to suffer for the glory of Christ

"Therefore, since Christ suffered in his body, arm yourselves also with the same attitude, because whoever suffers in the body is done with sin. As a result, they do not live the rest of their earthly lives for evil human desires, but rather for the will of God" (1 Peter 4:1–2).

It is not necessarily "natural" for us to do things God's way, especially if we are used to doing things our way—the way we have always done them—such as acting foolishly or being vengeful. Following the Lord completely means following Him in every area—including in the way we make decisions. Since His way is the right way, for us to pursue what is natural to us may lead to making disastrous decisions that result in regret.

> "There is a way that appears to be right, but in the end it leads to death."
> (Proverbs 14:12)

▶ Do you wait too long before asking God to show you His will?

▶ Do you ask everyone you know for advice instead of asking God?

▶ Do you fail to look at the big picture?

▶ Do you lie about failure, whether big or small?

▶ Do you ignore or minimize the impact your decision will have on others?

▶ Do you make choices too quickly?

▶ Do you fail to weigh the pros and cons of a specific action?

▶ Do you fail to explore other options?

▶ Do you take action prematurely before making necessary plans?

▶ Do you overlook the moral implications of a decision?

"The wise in heart are called discerning,
and gracious words promote instruction."
(Proverbs 16:21)

QUESTION: "What can I do when the way seems dark about a decision that must be made?"

ANSWER: Many times the Bible speaks specifically to a circumstance in your life. At other times, you must look for guiding biblical principles that can light your way.

"Your word is a lamp for my feet,
a light on my path."
(Psalm 119:105)

WHAT CAUSES Decision Making Delay?

Typically, procrastinators who don't intend to procrastinate do not understand themselves at all. On a continuum from mild to extreme, this negative pattern of behavior is an outgrowth of five "personality types."

These five types of unintentional procrastinators put off doing what should be done because of one or more of these five underlying root causes.

1 Perfectionism

2 Poor self-worth

3 Fear

4 Lack-of-goals

5 Feeling overwhelmed

Procrastination is both debilitating and habit forming. Unintentional procrastinators want to change but don't know how to change. Eventually, wave after wave of hopelessness overtakes them. However, if they can gain wisdom about themselves and about God's plan for them, not only can their lives be changed, but their futures can also be full of hope. The Bible says ...

"Know also that wisdom is like honey for you: If you find it, there is a future hope for you, and your hope will not be cut off."
(Proverbs 24:14)

Who Are the Five Procrastinators?

▶ PERFECTIONIST PATTY

- Overly emphasizing what she does—not who she is—Patty feels paralyzed because she can't measure up to the unrealistic standards she sets for herself. She feels she must perform perfectly, yet is stymied when she discovers that perfection is unattainable! With such a mind-set, who wouldn't suffer the paralysis of procrastination? Patty puts impossible expectations on herself, only to find that her self-worth suffers. Her "inner critic" is her constant companion.

- **Patty's Thinking**: Thrives on "performance-based acceptance"

"I must do this perfectly. Anything short of perfection is failure."

- **Patty's Feeling**: Hard worker, hardest on herself

"If it's not perfect, I'll feel horrible."

- **Patty's Response**: Involved in self-deception, prerequisites must be in place

"I can't start until I have everything just right."

- **Patty's Assumption**: Procrastinates because of not wanting to appear imperfect

"If I do it perfectly, I'll be accepted. I won't be rejected."

- **Conclusion**: Perfectionist Patty procrastinates because she is never satisfied with her performance. She doesn't realize that God doesn't demand perfection. He desires only that she aim for excellence. Patty needs to be at peace in her times of stress and learn to rely on His strength. The Lord says ...

**"My grace is sufficient for you,
for my power is made perfect in weakness."
(2 Corinthians 12:9)**

▶ POOR SELF-WORTH PAUL

- Overcontrolled by what others think and thinking so poorly of himself, Paul struggles just to get started. Since in his heart he doesn't feel acceptable, he assumes that nothing he does will be acceptable. Paul's negative self-talk makes any goal unattainable. He tends to think, *So why try?* When he makes mistakes, rather than learning lessons and persevering through to completion, his low self-worth weighs him down, and he simply gives up trying.

- **Paul's Thinking**: Early messages of inadequacy

  "I just can't do this."

- **Paul's Feeling**: Feels he has no real value; feels inadequate

  "I feel so insignificant, so incapable, so unnecessary."

- **Paul's Response**: Compares himself to others, remains passive

  "I'm not good enough to succeed. There's no sense in trying."

- **Paul's Assumption**: Procrastinates because of feeling inferior

  "I'm sure I will fail."

- **Conclusion**: Poor Self-worth Paul procrastinates because he lacks God's perspective of his value. Paul can't see what he is capable of achieving. He doesn't realize that God not only created him, but also preplanned the work He designed Paul to do. The Bible says ...

"We are God's handiwork, created in Christ Jesus to do good works, which God prepared in advance for us to do."
(Ephesians 2:10)

▶ **FEAR-BASED FREDDIE**

- Overly afraid that people and circumstances can't be trusted, Freddie sees life as risky and sidesteps responsibility in order to feel safe. When faced with an assignment, he feels anxious. *What if I make a costly mistake?* Freddie's fear prevents him from following through with a task because he expects a negative reaction from others. Freddie's procrastination is *focused* not only on his own performance—which he knows is flawed—but also on the opinions of others, which he knows will be condemning.

- **Freddie's Thinking**: Classic worrier

   "I know I won't succeed and that would be horrible!"

- **Freddie's Feeling**: Afraid of confrontation, fear of conflict takes control

   "I dread starting something that might go wrong and cause conflict."

- **Freddie's Response**: Puts off anything that could evoke a negative reaction

  "I'm afraid to start because I'm sure to fail."

- **Freddie's Assumption**: Procrastinates because of fear of conflict

  "If I put it off, I won't have to deal with it."

- **Conclusion**: Fear-based Freddie procrastinates because he believes any effort has the potential of bringing a rejection—if not an explosion! Freddie doesn't have to be controlled by fear because, even in stressful situations, he can claim ...

  > "In God I trust and am not afraid.
  > What can man do to me?"
  > (Psalm 56:11)

▶ Lack-of-Goals Larry

- Overly dependent on others for decision making, Larry has no real sense of purpose for his life. He hopes that one day his life will amount to something. But because Larry has no clear direction, he has difficulty setting goals, making decisions, and staying focused. His lack of purpose makes beginning any task a burden.

- **Larry's Thinking**: Ship without a rudder; can't steer because he has no map

  "I don't know why I am doing what I'm doing."

- **Larry's Feeling**: Lost because he doesn't know where he's going

"No matter what I do, I don't feel fulfilled."

- **Larry's Response**: Knows he needs to chart the course, but finds himself dead in the water

"Why start this task when it really doesn't make any difference?"

- **Larry's Assumption**: Procrastinates because of being directionless

"I need to wait until I can figure out what I really want to do."

- **Conclusion**: Lack-of-goals Larry delays accomplishing tasks because he is unable to see how any of his tasks contribute to a meaningful goal. Larry doesn't realize that God has planned a fulfilling course for him. The Bible says ...

> "Our people must learn to devote themselves to doing what is good, in order to provide for urgent needs and not live unproductive lives."
> (Titus 3:14)

▶ **OVERWHELMED OLIVIA**

- Overly committed to being a people pleaser, Olivia's work area looks like a disaster area. Her phone is lost under a pile of "to-do" lists. Someone is coming by in five minutes, but she is already ten minutes late for another meeting. She works feverishly, but finds no way to get on top of it all. There just isn't enough time in the day for her to do what she needs to do.

- **Olivia's Thinking**: Overcome with overload

  "I'm doing the best I can, but there's no way I can finish on time."

- **Olivia's Feeling**: Ill-equipped for handling tasks

  "My life feels out of control."

- **Olivia's Response**: Chooses easiest tasks first over the most important

  "Since I can't get it all done on time, I'll work on a project that I really enjoy and at least accomplish something."

- **Olivia's Assumption**: Procrastinates because of being on overload

  "I just need to work harder and faster somehow."

- **Conclusion**: Overwhelmed Olivia procrastinates because she feels responsible for more than she can handle, yet has no ability to manage her time in a meaningful way. Olivia doesn't realize that she has all the time she truly needs because God will never require more of her than she can do. Olivia needs to take these verses to heart ...

" ... the wise heart will know
the proper time and procedure.
For there is a proper time
and procedure for every matter ... "
(Ecclesiastes 8:5–6)

Procrastination vs. Postponement

QUESTION: "Is it ever right to procrastinate intentionally and postpone working on a task?"

ANSWER: Procrastination of a task and postponing a task are not necessarily the same. You may have legitimate reasons for postponing a task.

You need to delay a task when ...

▶ It isn't your highest priority.

▶ It will keep you from a previous commitment.

▶ It will compromise your health.

▶ It appears urgent, but it isn't important.

▶ It is important, but you are not the one to do it.

▶ It is you who should do it, but beginning now would be premature.

Be aware that doing a task could be right, but the timing could be wrong.

"Desire without knowledge is not good—
how much more will hasty feet
miss the way!"
(Proverbs 19:2)

Scripture warns against those who come to us in sheep's clothing but who are really ravenous wolves seeking to devour us. Their promises are empty, and they set all kinds of snares to trap us and take us prey. Some of those snares are promises of prosperity and prestige, power and popularity, or instant gratification and glory. All these promises are based on deception and all offer a false sense of security—the empty hope of perpetual prosperity and pleasure.

Too many trusting people have been taken captive to these lies and have fallen headlong into a belief system that says you are entitled to only good things and not bad; that you can expect life to always go your way; that if you have enough faith and pray in the name of Jesus, then God will answer every prayer as you desire; that God will meet not only your every need but also your every want—and do it in a timely fashion. These so-called spiritual leaders have pushed aside the true sovereign Decision Maker and established themselves as lord not only over their own lives but also over the lives of others.

Such arrogance leads to "expectation-based decision making," which leads to disappointment, delusion, and sometimes utter destruction. Our hope should not be placed in that which has been created but in the One who creates, in God, the Creator, Sustainer, and Sovereign Ruler of heaven and earth and all who dwell therein. The Bible describes those who were darkened in their understanding—those who ...

> " ... exchanged the truth about God for a lie, and worshiped and served created things rather than the Creator ... " (Romans 1:25)

In this age of unparalleled accomplishments and unimaginable progress in multiplied areas, expectations for what humanity can comprehend and accomplish have soared beyond our wildest imaginings with even the sky no longer setting the limit. With seemingly unlimited options comes unrestrained expectations in almost all areas of life. People have come to expect ...

▶ **Possessions**: Luxury cars, designer clothes, large houses

▶ **Employment**: High income, safe investments, guaranteed retirement

▶ **Government Aid**: Monetary entitlements, health and food benefits, guaranteed housing

▶ **Education**: Paved road to prosperity, solid foundation for a good job, open door to successful careers

▶ **Relationships**: Sexually, socially, intellectually, and emotionally gratifying, trouble-free and maintenance free, disposable and recyclable

▶ **Parenthood**: Ego-building, undemanding and stress-free, conditional rather than unconditional commitment

High expectations reflect excessive pride and selfishness and result in decision making governed by self-gain—what is in our interest and not in the interest of others, least of all God and His will. The result is laid out in the book of James:

> "If you harbor bitter envy and selfish ambition in your hearts,
> do not boast about it or deny the truth.
> Such 'wisdom' does not come down from heaven but is earthly, unspiritual, demonic.
> For where you have envy and selfish ambition, there you find disorder
> and every evil practice."
> (James 3:14–16)

As the Scriptures indicate, when decisions carry with them expectations of people, government, employment, society, circumstances, and especially God, it is a setup for a disappointing and disastrous outcome.

▶ **DECISION**: "I'll give a very nice present."

- **Expectation**: Gratitude, reciprocity, and loyalty

- **Outcome**: Little thanks, no gift in return, and disloyalty

  Instead Jesus said, *"It is more blessed to give than to receive"* (Acts 20:35).

▶ **DECISION**: "I'll spend the day doing whatever she wants me to do."

- **Expectation**: Praise and freedom to do whatever you want to do on another day.

- **Outcome**: Little appreciation and a longer list of chores to perform

  Instead Philippians 2:3 says, *"Do nothing out of selfish ambition or vain conceit. Rather, in humility value others above yourselves"* (Philippians 2:3).

▶ **DECISION**: "I'll help out a fellow church member in great financial need."

  - **Expectation**: Recognition at church and admiration of fellow members

  - **Outcome**: No public acknowledgment of good deed and no pats on the back

    Instead Jesus said, *"So when you give to the needy, do not announce it with trumpets, as the hypocrites do in the synagogues and on the streets, to be honored by others. Truly I tell you, they have received their reward in full. But when you give to the needy, do not let your left hand know what your right hand is doing, so that your giving may be in secret. Then your Father, who sees what is done in secret, will reward you"* (Matthew 6:2–4).

▶ **DECISION**: "I'll extend forgiveness for wrongs committed against me."

  - **Expectation**: Confession, repentance, and humility from offender

  - **Outcome**: Prideful response, denial of wrongdoing, and no repentance

Instead Peter asked Jesus, *"'Lord, how many times shall I forgive my brother or sister who sins against me? Up to seven times?' Jesus answered, 'I tell you, not seven times, but seventy-seven times'"* (Matthew 18:21–22).

▶ **DECISION**: "I'll make a generous donation to a Christian ministry."

- **Expectation**: Financial windfall or other material blessing from God

- **Outcome**: Unexpected financial reversal, illness, automobile trouble

  Instead Jesus said, *"Be careful not to practice your righteousness in front of others to be seen by them. If you do, you will have no reward from your Father in heaven"* (Matthew 6:1).

▶ **DECISION**: "I'll work after hours, take on added responsibilities, flatter the boss."

- **Expectation**: Promotion, pay raise, recognition, job security

- **Outcome**: No financial compensation, increased demands, and greater pressure to perform above job requirements

  Instead Jesus said, *"Just as the Son of Man did not come to be served, but to serve, and to give his life as a ransom for many"* (Matthew 20:28).

Rather than being in bondage to expectations and basing our decisions on desired outcomes that are dependent on the decisions of others, God wants us to trust Him with the ramifications of our decisions. He is trustworthy, and His promises of an eternal reward for godly choices are certain. His words to us today are the same as the words He spoke to His disciples over 2,000 years ago:

> "Whoever serves me must follow me;
> and where I am, my servant also will be.
> My Father will honor the one
> who serves me." (John 12:26)

ROOT CAUSE for Anxiety Over Decisions

Swords at their side and moving down the mountain, David and his men encounter a figure prostrate before them—Nabal's wife, Abigail. Tipped off by a shepherd about the impending massacre, the discerning wife of Nabal turns *diplomatic* and sends on ahead of her a feast on four legs: an entourage of donkeys laden down with two hundred loaves of bread, wine, five prepared sheep, grain, a hundred clusters of raisins, and two hundred fig cakes. As soon as she sees David, she wastes no time dismounting her donkey and falling at his feet to appeal for mercy for her household and restraint for David's men. She expresses her disdain for Nabal's folly, offers his men food, and honors David with words befitting a king.

> "David said to Abigail, 'Praise be to the LORD, the God of Israel, who has sent you today to meet me. May you be blessed for your good judgment and for keeping me from bloodshed this day and from avenging myself with my own hands.'"
> (1 Samuel 25:32–33)

Abigail wisely decided she had to act quickly because of the foolish decisions of her husband. What a contrast in decision making!

Three God-Given Inner Needs

In reality, we have all been created with three God-given inner needs: the needs for love, significance, and security.[7]

▶ **Love**—to know that someone is unconditionally committed to our best interest

"My command is this: Love each other as I have loved you" (John 15:12).

▶ **Significance**—to know that our lives have meaning and purpose

"I cry out to God Most High, to God who fulfills his purpose for me" (Psalm 57:2 ESV).

▶ **Security**—to feel accepted and a sense of belonging

"Whoever fears the LORD has a secure fortress, and for their children it will be a refuge" (Proverbs 14:26).

The Ultimate Need-Meeter

Why did God give us these deep inner needs, knowing that people fail people and self-effort fails us as well?

God gave us these inner needs so that we would come to know Him as our Need-Meeter. Our needs are designed by God to draw us into a deeper dependence on Christ. God did not create any person or position, or any amount of power or possessions to meet the deepest needs in our lives. If a person or thing could meet all our needs, we wouldn't need God! The Lord will use circumstances and bring positive people into our lives as an extension of His care and compassion, but ultimately only God can satisfy all the needs of our hearts.

The Bible says ...

> "The LORD will guide you always;
> he will satisfy your needs in a sun-scorched
> land and will strengthen your frame.
> You will be like a well-watered garden,
> like a spring whose waters never fail."
> (Isaiah 58:11)

The apostle Paul revealed this truth by first asking, *"What a wretched man I am. Who will rescue me from this body that is subject to death?"* and then by answering his own question in saying it is " ... *Jesus Christ our Lord!"* (Romans 7:24–25).

All along, the Lord planned to meet our deepest needs for ...

▶ **Love**—*"I [the Lord] have loved you with an everlasting love; I have drawn you with unfailing kindness"* (Jeremiah 31:3).

▶ **Significance**—*"'For I know the plans I have for you,' declares the LORD, 'plans to prosper you and not to harm you, plans to give you hope and a future'"* (Jeremiah 29:11).

▶ **Security**—*"The LORD himself goes before you and will be with you; he will never leave you nor forsake you. Do not be afraid; do not be discouraged"* (Deuteronomy 31:8).

The truth is that our God-given needs for love, significance, and security can be legitimately met in Christ Jesus! Philippians 4:19 makes it plain: *"My God will meet all your needs according to the riches of his glory in Christ Jesus."*

▶ **WRONG BELIEF:**

"I can't trust God with all of my decisions in life. I need to rely on my own abilities to influence an outcome that I desire."

▶ **RIGHT BELIEF:**

"God will come through for me when I step out in faith and trust Him to guide me in all decisions."

> "Trust in the LORD with all your heart
> and lean not on your own understanding;
> in all your ways submit to him, and he will
> make your paths straight. Do not be wise in
> your own eyes; fear the LORD and shun evil."
> (Proverbs 3:5–7)

Abigail's actions demonstrate a right belief, taking a giant step of faith because she trusted God to intervene and help in a most desperate situation. God indeed meets all of her needs, and she is richly rewarded for decision making rooted in a knowledge of His ways and plans.

> *The more you choose to please God,*
> *the more you will discern*
> *the will of God.*

STEPS TO SOLUTION

Chicken Little, the classic children's fable, demonstrates the potential consequence of making a decision based on fear. When the falling acorn hit her head, the little hen ran from one friend to another exclaiming, "The sky is falling, the sky is falling! Oh, what will we do?" One by one, her barnyard friends became alarmed and narrowly escaped being eaten by the fox as they ran to tell the king.

This same kind of fear is demonstrated when people panic over the future uncertainty of "What will we do?" God's direction is not always obvious because He is more concerned with *what we become* rather than with *what we do*! His goal is the process, developing our character and deepening our knowledge of His ways.

" ... this is my prayer: that your love may abound more and more in knowledge and depth of insight, so that you may be able to discern what is best and may be pure and blameless for the day of Christ."
(Philippians 1:9–10)

Key Passage to Read

1 Thessalonians 4:1–12—Living to Please God

▶ **Live** your life choosing to please God in all you do. (v. 1)

▶ **Live** by growing in the knowledge of God's ways—study the Bible. (vv. 1–2)

▶ **Live** a life that is "set apart" from the ways of the world. (v. 3)

▶ **Live** within God's requirements for sexual purity. (v. 3)

▶ **Live** a life that demonstrates self-control. (v. 4)

▶ **Live** a life that is holy and honorable. (vv. 4, 7)

▶ **Live** without lusting like pagans. (v. 5)

▶ **Live** with integrity in relationships with others. (v. 6)

- ▶ **Live** knowing that when you reject the Word of God, you reject God. (v. 8)

- ▶ **Live** with brotherly love toward others. (vv. 9–10)

- ▶ **Live** a quiet life, minding your own affairs. (v. 11)

- ▶ **Live** a life that gains the respect of others. (v. 12)

- ▶ **Live** a life that is dependent on no one except the Lord. (v. 12)

THE MOST Important Decision of Your Life

Never has there been a time when divine guidance wasn't desired. The ancient world was consumed with the pursuit of spiritual knowledge and power. Yet the road traveled was strewn with pagan rituals, sacrifices, omens, and astrology. Amazingly, people today are still infatuated with seeking God's guidance through similar occult practices even though the Bible clearly states such methods are abhorrent.

"Let no one be found among you who sacrifices their son or daughter in the fire, who practices divination or sorcery, interprets omens, engages in witchcraft, or casts spells, or who is a medium or spiritist or who consults the dead. Anyone who does these things is detestable

to the LORD; because of these same detestable practices the LORD your God will drive out those nations before you."
(Deuteronomy 18:10–12)

When you come to a crossroad in life where knowing God's will is crucial, don't look for signs in the sky! The worst decision you can make is to go against God's will—and to reject Jesus as your personal Lord and Savior. There is only one way to gain true wisdom—through God Himself. Today you can have direct access to God! He has made a way for you to know Him and to know His will for your life.

The first step to having this kind of relationship is submitting to the sovereignty of God. Admit that you've been the major decision maker, and then willingly surrender your will to the will of the Lord—let Him be your personal Decision Maker for the rest of your life.

How to Make the Most Important Decision

Four points you need to know:

#1 God's Purpose for You is *Salvation.*

What was God's motivation in sending Jesus Christ to earth?

To express His love for you by saving you! The Bible says ...

"God so loved the world that he gave his one and

only Son, that whoever believes in him shall not perish but have eternal life. For God did not send his Son into the world to condemn the world, but to save the world through him" (John 3:16–17).

What was Jesus' purpose in coming to earth?

To forgive your sins, to empower you to have victory over sin, and to enable you to live a fulfilled life! Jesus said ...

"I have come that they may have life, and that they may have it more abundantly" (John 10:10 NKJV).

#2 Your Problem is *Sin*.

What exactly is sin?

Sin is living independently of God's standard—knowing what is right, but choosing what is wrong. The Bible says ...

"If anyone, then, knows the good they ought to do and doesn't do it, it is sin for them" (James 4:17).

What is the major consequence of sin?

Spiritual death, eternal separation from God. Scripture states ...

"Your iniquities [sins] have separated you from your God. ... The wages of sin is death, but the gift of God is eternal life in Christ Jesus our Lord" (Isaiah 59:2; Romans 6:23).

#3 God's Provision for You is the *Savior.*

Can anything remove the penalty for sin?

Yes! Jesus died on the cross to personally pay the penalty for your sins. The Bible says ...

"God demonstrates his own love for us in this: While we were still sinners, Christ died for us" (Romans 5:8).

What is the solution to being separated from God?

Belief in (entrusting your life to) Jesus Christ as the only way to God the Father. Jesus says ...

"I am the way and the truth and the life. No one comes to the Father except through me. ... Believe in the Lord Jesus, and you will be saved" (John 14:6; Acts 16:31).

#4 Your Part is *Surrender.*

Give Christ control of your life, entrusting yourself to Him.

"Jesus said to his disciples, 'Whoever wants to be my disciple must deny themselves and take up their cross [die to your own self-rule] and follow me. For whoever wants to save their life will lose it, but whoever loses their life for me will find it. What good will it be for someone to gain the whole world, yet forfeit their soul?'" (Matthew 16:24–26).

Place your faith in (rely on) Jesus Christ as your personal Lord and Savior and reject your "good works" as a means of earning God's approval. ...

"It is by grace you have been saved, through faith—and this is not from yourselves, it is the gift of God—not by works, so that no one can boast" (Ephesians 2:8–9).

The moment you choose to receive Jesus as your Lord and Savior—entrusting your life to Him— He comes to live inside you. Then He gives you His power to live the fulfilled life God has planned for you.

If you want to be fully forgiven by God and become the person God created you to be, you can tell Him in a simple, heartfelt prayer like this:

PRAYER OF SALVATION

God, I want a real relationship with You.
I admit that many times I've failed
to go Your way and instead
chosen to go my own way.
Please forgive me for my sins.
Jesus, thank You for dying on the cross
to pay the penalty for my sins and for rising
from the dead to provide new life.
Come into my life to be my Lord
and my Savior.
Place Your hope in my heart
and teach me to put my confidence in You.
Make me the person You created me to be.
In Your holy name I pray.
Amen.

What Can You Expect Now?

If you sincerely prayed this prayer, know that God will give you *His wisdom* to make the best decisions, the ones that accomplish *His will* for your life!

"If any of you lacks wisdom, you should ask God, who gives generously to all without finding fault, and it will be given to you."
(James 1:5)

HOW TO Reach the Target

When Christ enters the human heart, He brings a new purpose, establishes a new priority, and lays out a new plan. These three targets become the focal point of the person's new life in Christ.

"Therefore, if anyone is in Christ,
the new creation has come:
The old has gone, the new is here!"
(2 Corinthians 5:17)

Reaching the Target

▶ **Target #1—A New Purpose**: God's purpose for me is to be conformed to the character of Christ.

"Those God foreknew he also predestined to be conformed to the image of his Son ... " (Romans 8:29).

- "I'll do whatever it takes to be conformed to the character of Christ."

▶ **Target #2—A New Priority**: God's priority for me is to change my thinking.

"Do not conform to the pattern of this world, but be transformed by the renewing of your mind" (Romans 12:2).

- "I'll do whatever it takes to line up my thinking with God's thinking."

▶ **Target #3—A New Plan**: God's plan for me is to rely on Christ's strength, not my strength, to be all He created me to be.

"I can do all things through him who strengthens me" (Philippians 4:13 ESV).

- "I'll do whatever it takes to fulfill His plan in His strength."

My Personalized Plan for Sound Decision Making

As I determine in my heart to become the person God created me to be, I will seek the leading of the Holy Spirit in formulating a plan that will help me to rely on His strength within me, not on my own abilities. I will make it my goal to ...

▶ **Seek** God's will first and foremost

- Read and study Scripture to better understand the character and ways of God

- Pray fervently for wisdom and direction in all I do

- Pursue godly counsel when God's will is not obvious

- Discern how God might be using circumstances to lead or direct me

"Get wisdom, get understanding; do not forget my words or turn away from them" (Proverbs 4:5).

▶ **Be** "decisive" about being decisive

- Allow faith, not fear, to prevail through memorizing verses that strengthen my faith

- Avoid procrastination by making a weekly schedule for taking care of specific responsibilities

- Refrain from making decisions solely to please others

- Permit the presence of God's peace to give me confidence by consistently reminding myself that He is always with me

"God is faithful, who has called you into fellowship with his Son, Jesus Christ our Lord" (1 Corinthians 1:9).

▶ **Flee** from false, ungodly counsel

- Turn a deaf ear to counsel from occult sources, such as astrologers and psychics

- Reject any counsel that advises relying on intuition or instinct

- Renounce all counsel that violates biblical principles

- Refuse to be persuaded by those who question God's "best" for my life

"Blessed is the one who does not walk in step with the wicked or stand in the way that sinners take or sit in the company of mockers" (Psalm 1:1).

▶ **Practice** sound judgment

- Commit to never let feelings alone be the driving factor in decision making

- Assess any personal motives behind the decisions I need to make

- Carefully weigh all sides of an issue before making a decision

- Execute decisions with diligence and fairness

"The fear of the LORD is the beginning of wisdom, and knowledge of the Holy One is understanding" (Proverbs 9:10).

HOW TO Develop Spiritual Discernment

Just as discernment does not come by flipping a coin and saying "heads or tails," neither does it completely rely on common sense or the conscience. Spiritual discernment is a gift from God and comes to us through the Holy Spirit, who dwells in every authentic Christian. It is the supernatural ability to "know" something not because of personal knowledge or experience, but because of personal time spent in God's Word and in prayer with Him.

"If any of you lacks wisdom,
you should ask God, who gives generously
to all without finding fault, and it will be
given to you. But when you ask, you must
believe and not doubt, because the one who
doubts is like a wave of the sea, blown and
tossed by the wind. That person should not
expect to receive anything from the Lord."
(James 1:5–7)

The ability to know God and discern His will for your life comes through ...

▶ **Salvation**

- Spiritual things can be discerned only by the indwelling Spirit of Christ. When you have trusted Jesus as your Lord and Savior and have begun a personal relationship with Him, you have met the prerequisite for knowing *"the mind of Christ."*

  "The person with the Spirit makes judgments about all things, but such a person is not subject to merely human judgments, for, 'Who has known the mind of the Lord so as to instruct him?' But we have the mind of Christ." (1 Corinthians 2:15–16).

▶ **Scripture**

- As you study Scripture, you learn how God works in the lives of His people. Understanding God's principles gives you a basis for knowing how He is working in your life today.

"The fear of the LORD is the beginning of wisdom; all who follow his precepts have good understanding. To him belongs eternal praise" (Psalm 111:10).

"These things happened to them as examples and were written down as warnings for us, on whom the culmination of the ages has come" (1 Corinthians 10:11).

▶ Situations

- Are you focusing on "What is God's will for my future?" Instead, focus on God's purpose in your present situation, and trust Him with your future. God always has a personal will for you, and your responsibility is to adjust to what He is doing in your life right now.

  "... seek first his kingdom and his righteousness, and all these things will be given to you as well. Therefore do not worry about tomorrow, for tomorrow will worry about itself. Each day has enough trouble of its own" (Matthew 6:33–34).

▶ Submission

- Are you submitting to what God wants to do in your life today? Pray to be moldable clay in the Potter's hand, allowing God to mold and shape you into the vessel of His choosing.

  "'Can I not do with you, Israel, as this potter does?' declares the LORD. 'Like clay in the hand of the potter, so are you in my hand, Israel'" (Jeremiah 18:6).

▶ Servanthood

- Have you given up ownership of your own life? When your heart is willing to be God's servant no matter the cost, He will reveal His plan for you.

"No one can serve two masters. Either you will hate the one and love the other, or you will be devoted to the one and despise the other. You cannot serve both God and money. Therefore I tell you, do not worry about your life, what you will eat or drink; or about your body, what you will wear. Is not life more than food, and the body more than clothes?" (Matthew 6:24–25).

DISCERN THE Spirit's Leading

When you experience authentic salvation by recognizing your sin and separation from God and accepting Christ's death as payment for your personal sins, God sends His Holy Spirit to abide within your human spirit. In this way, God will guide you into all truth and prompt you to cooperate in bringing about His purposes for your life.

" ... when he, the Spirit of truth, comes, he will guide you into all the truth.
He will not speak on his own;
he will speak only what he hears, and he will tell you what is yet to come." (John 16:13)

▶ The soul is made up of the mind, the will, and the emotions.[8] As the Holy Spirit relates to your soul:

- He teaches your *mind* how to *think*.

- He directs your *will* how to *act*.

- He brings your *emotions* into *alignment* (what is right in God's sight).

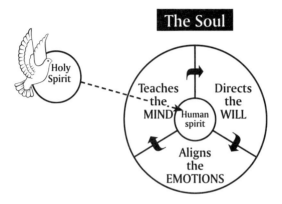

The Soul

Holy Spirit

Teaches the MIND

Human spirit

Directs the WILL

Aligns the EMOTIONS

▶ When faced with a decision or deadline—tell God that you want only His will.

- Ask God to shut all doors to opportunities that are not His choice.

- Ask God for a heavy heart if you are making the wrong choice and peace if you are making the right choice.

"'What no eye has seen,
what no ear has heard, and what no human
mind has conceived'—the things God has
prepared for those who love him—
these are the things God has revealed to us
by his Spirit. The Spirit searches all things,
even the deep things of God."
(1 Corinthians 2:9–10)

"Doing what comes naturally" is not a good barometer for determining God's will in your life. What comes naturally can be the sinful nature or the "flesh," which operates apart from the Spirit of God. How can you determine whether what you think you should do reflects God's will or whether it is your own natural wishes and desires?

"For the flesh desires what is contrary to the Spirit, and the Spirit what is contrary to the flesh. They are in conflict with each other, so that you are not to do whatever you want." (Galatians 5:17)

▶ **Don't** wait until all else fails before seeking God's will.

"But Jehoshaphat also said to the king of Israel, 'First seek the counsel of the LORD'" (1 Kings 22:5).

▶ **Don't** seek the plan but rather the Person who reveals the plan.

"Trust in the LORD with all your heart and lean not on your own understanding; in all your ways submit to him, and he will make your paths straight" (Proverbs 3:5–6).

▶ **Don't** pray for permission regarding something God has forbidden.

"I have taken an oath and confirmed it, that I will follow your righteous laws" (Psalm 119:106).

▶ **Don't** make decisions based on feelings.

"Above all else, guard your heart, for everything you do flows from it" (Proverbs 4:23).

▶ **Don't** assume that God's will is too difficult for you to do.

"In fact, this is love for God: to keep his commands. And his commands are not burdensome" (1 John 5:3).

▶ **Don't** have divided loyalty and allow money to dictate your decision.

"No one can serve two masters. Either you will hate the one and love the other, or you will be devoted to the one and despise the other. You cannot serve both God and money" (Matthew 6:24).

▶ **Don't** test God by seeking visible signs.

"Do not put the LORD your God to the test as you did at Massah" (Deuteronomy 6:16).

▶ **Don't** think that trials and adversity indicate you are out of God's will.

"So then, those who suffer according to God's will should commit themselves to their faithful Creator and continue to do good" (1 Peter 4:19).

"Gut" Feelings

QUESTION: "Sometimes I have a 'gut feeling' about a situation. But, can a 'gut feeling' actually be from God?"

ANSWER: Yes, but beware: A bad "gut feeling" could be the result of a bad piece of pizza! Realize, if you need to know God's will about any decision, God can use *any method* to speak to you. After all, He's been known to use a burning bush, a dramatic dream, and even a donkey.

As long as you continue to commit your life to the Lord—yielding your will to His will—if you have a "gut feeling" about something or someone, then you can probably "trust your gut." Meaning, more than likely, the Spirit of God is giving you that "gut feeling." Jesus explained to His disciples that after His death, the Spirit of Truth would come to them. ...

"The Advocate, the Holy Spirit,
whom the Father will send in my name,
will teach you all things and will remind you
of everything I have said to you."
(John 14:26)

Making decisions based on presumptive expectations of ourselves and others is unwise because it sets us up to be disappointed, discouraged, and disillusioned. That is not to say that we shouldn't consider the *impact* of our choices on ourselves and others, because we need always to weigh the cost of our choices.

However, having expectations of people puts us at their mercy in the sense that we are powerless over the decisions others make. To choose a course of action based on the expectation that it will bring about some desired outcome is not the basis on which God wants us to make decisions.

Our decisions are to be led by Him and not by selfish desires. Our desire in decision making is to please God by following His will for our lives. Decision making is an exercise in trusting God by choosing to follow Him. It is free of any expectation except that of glorifying God by yielding our will to His will. Just as Jesus based His decisions on His Father's will for Him, we are to base our decisions on His will for us.

"For I did not speak on my own,
but the Father who sent me commanded me
to say all that I have spoken.
I know that his command leads to eternal
life. So whatever I say is just what the Father
has told me to say. ... Don't you believe that
I am in the Father, and that the Father is in

me? The words I say to you I do not speak on my own authority. Rather, it is the Father, living in me, who is doing his work. ... Again Jesus said, 'Peace be with you! As the Father has sent me, I am sending you.'" (John 12:49–50; 14:10; 20:21)

As you seek to eliminate attaching expectations to decisions you make, consider following the example of Christ.

▶ **Accept** your limitations and the limitations of others.

- Jesus did not heal or disciple everyone.

- Jesus satisfied His physical need for food and rest.

- Jesus knew the hearts of men and fully depended only on His Father.

"And my God will meet all your needs according to the riches of his glory in Christ Jesus" (Philippians 4:19).

▶ **Find** contentment in the everyday blessings of God.

- Pursue the kingdom of God, not worldly wealth or fame.

- Enjoy the simple pleasures of life, such as fellowship with friends.

- Expect suffering and use it to learn obedience.

"I am not saying this because I am in need, for I have learned to be content whatever

the circumstances. I know what it is to be in need, and I know what it is to have plenty. I have learned the secret of being content in any and every situation, whether well fed or hungry, whether living in plenty or in want" (Philippians 4:11–12).

▶ **Redefine** happiness according to God's definition.

- Practice the Beatitudes Christ taught in the Sermon on the Mount.

- Focus on people, not on possessions.

- Find inner sustenance in spiritual food.

"Keep your lives free from the love of money and be content with what you have, because God has said, 'Never will I leave you; never will I forsake you'" (Hebrews 13:5).

▶ **Shun** the snare of power and prestige.

- Lay aside your "right" to exert your authority over others.

- Surrender your will to God and submit to His authority.

- Use your position of influence to benefit others.

"Then he said to them, 'Watch out! Be on your guard against all kinds of greed; life does not consist in an abundance of possessions'" (Luke 12:15).

▶ **Don't pursue** that which is "bigger and better."

- Be generous in sharing God's provisions with others.

- Avoid making meaningless comparisons.

- View your belongings as the Lord's possessions.

"The earth is the LORD's, and everything in it, the world, and all who live in it" (Psalm 24:1).

▶ **Steer** clear of "sandy foundations."

- Establish your life on godly principles, not on worldly values.

- Invest your energy in people, not in projects.

- Give yourself to God while investing in people.

"Let no debt remain outstanding, except the continuing debt to love one another, for whoever loves others has fulfilled the law" (Romans 13:8).

DISCOVER GOD'S Guidance

Far too often we rely on our own instincts in making decisions. When a crisis occurs, we are confused because we have not consistently sought to understand how God guides. Trust that God is ultimately involved in every detail of your life. Listen, learn, and obtain His guidance.

" ... let the wise listen and add to their learning, and let the discerning get guidance." (Proverbs 1:5)

Gifts

▶ Discover and use the spiritual gifts, talents, and abilities God has given you to serve others. Discern His direction by noticing the opportunities He brings to develop those gifts.

- Reflect on what you really enjoy doing.

- Write down past accomplishments that have brought you joy.

- Become aware of your weaknesses.

- Ask a friend to evaluate your strengths.

"Each of you should use whatever gift you have received to serve others, as faithful stewards of God's grace in its various forms" (1 Peter 4:10).

Understanding

▶ Take time to clearly discern what the decision is about and what is involved.

- Do I know all the facts?

- Am I aware of the consequences of my choices?

- Is there a deadline for the decision?

- Am I making a decision based on guilt?

"Folly brings joy to one who has no sense, but whoever has understanding keeps a straight course" (Proverbs 15:21).

Impressions

▶ The Spirit of God often brings conviction or establishes truth in your heart through strong impressions of His thoughts or principles regarding a matter.

- Pray for God to speak to you about the matter.

- Consider a time of fasting if led to do so.

- Spend time in quiet reflection and meditation, seeking God's heart on the situation.

- Ask God to confirm your impression through another source.

"I will praise the LORD, who counsels me; even at night my heart instructs me" (Psalm 16:7).

Desires

▶ When you seek to please the Lord in all areas of your life, His desires will become the desires of your heart. As this occurs, His will in each situation becomes increasingly easier to recognize.

- Study Scripture to know the heart of God. Pray, "Lord, may I see my sin as You see it. May I hate my sin as You hate it."

- Find Scriptures that promise His strength for your weaknesses. Choose to believe them and thank Him.

"Take delight in the LORD, and he will give you the desires of your heart" (Psalm 37:4).

Advice

▶ God often speaks to us through others. Your wisdom is increased by seeking counsel from people who are ...

- Grounded in the Word of God

- Mature in godly wisdom

- Living successfully, having overcome similar circumstances

"Listen to advice and accept discipline, and at the end you will be counted among the wise" (Proverbs 19:20).

Necessity

▶ Evaluate your God-given responsibilities and choose your actions appropriately.

For example:

- If you have young children at home, decisions that would keep you from being with them for extended periods of time would not be in keeping with God's will for you.

- Moving a long distance away from a dependent, elderly parent who would be left alone would not be God's desire.

- Choosing to take a vacation at a time when your employer needed your assistance for an emergency is contrary to the biblical principle of having a submissive attitude toward those in authority over you.

"If anyone, then, knows the good they ought to do and doesn't do it, it is sin for them" (James 4:17).

Circumstances

▶ Not all doors are opened by God, but closed doors can help determine your way at least for the present.

- Circumstances are to be considered, but they are not the final answer.

- Learn to see beyond circumstances into what God wants to accomplish in your life now.

- When unsure about an "open door," pray for God to close the door if it is not His will for you.

"In their hearts humans plan their course, but the LORD establishes their steps" (Proverbs 16:9).

Elimination

▶ Even though all the choices may be permissible, some may not be the best.

- Eliminate one by one the options available to you.

- Eliminate choices that place you in tempting situations. (Don't go shopping if you're tempted to overspend.)

- Eliminate choices that would not be the best use of your time. (Don't organize a drawer when work on an assignment is past due.)

- Eliminate choices that require skills you don't have.

"'I have the right to do anything,' you say—but not everything is beneficial. 'I have the right to do anything'—but not everything is constructive" (1 Corinthians 10:23).

GOD'S PROMISES for Guidance

When faced with making a decision, look to God's Word for direction.

> **"Your word is a lamp for my feet,**
> **a light on my path."**
> **(Psalm 119:105)**

▶ Psalm 32:8

"I will instruct you and teach you in the way you should go; I will counsel you with my loving eye on you."

▶ Isaiah 42:16

"I will lead the blind by ways they have not known, along unfamiliar paths I will guide them; I will turn the darkness into light before them and make the rough places smooth. These are the things I will do; I will not forsake them."

▶ Psalm 37:23

"The LORD makes firm the steps of the one who delights in him."

▶ Proverbs 16:9

"In their hearts humans plan their course, but the LORD *establishes their steps."*

▶ Proverbs 3:5–6

"Trust in the LORD *with all your heart and lean not on your own understanding; in all your ways submit to him, and he will make your paths straight."*

▶ Isaiah 58:11

"The LORD *will guide you always; he will satisfy your needs in a sun-scorched land and will strengthen your frame. You will be like a well-watered garden, like a spring whose waters never fail."*

▶ Psalm 37:5–6

"Commit your way to the LORD*; trust in him and he will do this: He will make your righteous reward shine like the dawn, your vindication like the noonday sun."*

▶ Psalm 139:9–10

"If I rise on the wings of the dawn, if I settle on the far side of the sea, even there your hand will guide me, your right hand will hold me fast."

▶ Psalm 73:24

"You guide me with your counsel, and afterward you will take me into glory."

▶ Psalm 48:14

" … he will be our guide even to the end."

▶ John 16:13

" ... when he, the Spirit of truth, comes, he will guide you into all the truth. He will not speak on his own; he will speak only what he hears, and he will tell you what is yet to come."

▶ John 8:12

"I am the light of the world. Whoever follows me will never walk in darkness, but will have the light of life."

HOW TO Shrink the Stress of Endless Choices

Everywhere we turn there are choices to be made, some simple and some complex, some insignificant and some life-changing. Bottom line, many of us are overloaded with choices. Our brains are worn out from the stress of analyzing and making decisions. Sadly, some are so burned out by the end of the day that when they get home they abdicate their decision-making responsibility regarding the people they live with and love—their spouses and children.

The challenge for all of us caught in the dilemma of choice overload is to find a way to shrink the stress by decreasing the choices. Jesus offered the disciples advice that we would do well to follow today.

"And do not set your heart on what you will eat or drink; do not worry about it. For the pagan world runs after all such things, and your Father knows that you need them. But seek his kingdom, and these things will be given to you as well." (Luke 12:29–31)

Shrink Your Stress

As you seek to shrink the stress of having choice overload, choose to ...

▶ **Make** decisions only when necessary.

- Don't buy clothes if you have what is needed.

- Don't purchase trendy items that go out of style quickly.

- Mix and match your work wardrobe from clothes you already have.

- Plan meals around what family members like and what is in your pantry.

- Select meals on a weekly basis and limit purchases to only what is planned.

▶ **Establish** daily/weekly routines.

- Do your grocery shopping at the same store on the same day each week.

- Establish day and time for selected family fun activities.

- Set a specific time for serving evening meals.

- Select a day and time for regular family outings.

- Designate a particular day each week for taking care of errands and doing chores.

▶ **Stick** with previously made decisions.

- Don't make a decision and then revisit it on a regular basis.

- Identify and evaluate common every day choices, decide a course of action, and make them a family norm.

- Establish family rules or guidelines for choosing television programs, watching movies, selecting music, using computers and telephones.

- Set a weekly schedule of activities and don't change it.

- Declare at least two days a week as "no-decision-making" days.

▶ **Create** family and church traditions.

- Recognize the stability and security found in repetition of meaningful activities.

- Decide the valued and cherished practices enjoyed by family members and agree to make them family rituals.

- Encourage your church leadership to establish traditions that will add depth to relationships and enhance spiritual growth.

- Establish traditional celebrations of significant anniversary dates.

- Select some traditional activity for all holidays recognized by church, family, and/or friends.

▶ **Avoid** commercials, ads, telephone solicitations, etc.

- Accept that all marketing gimmicks are designed to get your money, not to meet your needs.

- Make a yearly budget for making donations and special purchases and honor it.

- Earmark the programs, ministries, and charities you will support financially for the year and evaluate all other requests for the following year.

- Set a designated amount to spend on "items-as-needed" and don't exceed that figure.

- Refuse to engage in any impulsive buying. Wait at least 24 to 48 hours before purchasing any item not specified in your budget.

▶ **Don't** replace what isn't broken.

- Realize that something new isn't always better than something old.

- Remember the wisdom behind the saying, "If it isn't broken, don't fix it."

- Refrain from paying for "extras" you don't really need when replacing a worn out appliance, car, computer, phone, or when changing one service provider for another.

- Refuse to be swayed by social pressure or the need to please people when it comes to spending your money—money God has provided.

- Recognize that we live in a "throw away" society but we have a God who holds us accountable for all He has given us, including even our food.

▶ **Take** responsibility for your decisions.

- Accept the fact that you are becoming the person and living the life of your own choosing.

- Realize that few of us are victims of our circumstances and that we are not deprived of choices unless we believe a lie and actively choose passivity over action.

- Understand that to not choose is still to choose, and we fool only ourselves when we say that we have no choice but to make ungodly decisions.

- Take charge of yourself and own your decisions, understanding that they define who you are as a person—your priorities, values, and character.

- Choose what your attitude toward life will be in the midst of the limits placed on you by work, family, society, circumstances, or friends.

- Recognize that life is a series of choices and that you alone can make the choices God has assigned to you—choices for which He holds you accountable—choices He desires to use to mold and shape you into the person He created you to be.

> "For those God foreknew he also predestined to be conformed to the image of his Son ... " (Romans 8:29)

WHEN TIME Has Run Out and You Still Don't Know What to Do

If you have to make a decision and you've prayed for God's choice, say to Him ...

"Lord, because You know everything, You know the decision before me and the way I should go. I want only Your will. Since I no longer have the option of waiting, I will choose (pick one of the options). If this decision is not right in Your sight, I ask Your Spirit in me to put a heaviness in my heart. If this is the right direction, please confirm it with Your peace. I am willing to take whatever detours You decide to put in my path, as long as I reach the destination You have for me. In Christ's name I pray. Amen."

> "I desire to do your will, my God; your law is within my heart." (Psalm 40:8)

God plays no game of hide-and-seek—
the closer you draw to the heart of God,
the more clearly you'll know
the will of God.
He reveals His will day by day.
He unrolls the scroll one line at a time.

—June Hunt

SCRIPTURES TO MEMORIZE

Who does God promise to **guide** and **teach His way?**

> *"He **guides** the humble in what is right, and **teaches** them **his way**."* (Psalm 25:9)

What really happens if I **trust in the Lord with all my heart?**

> *"**Trust in the LORD with all your heart** and lean not on your own understanding; in all your ways submit to him, and he will make your paths straight."* (Proverbs 3:5–6)

As I make decisions, what will shine **light on my path?**

> *"Your word is a lamp for my feet, a **light on my path**."* (Psalm 119:105)

How will God show me **the way I should go?**

> *"I will instruct you and teach you in **the way you should go**; I will counsel you with my loving eye on you."* (Psalm 32:8)

Can a person be **guided into all truth?**

> *"But when he, the Spirit of truth, comes, he will **guide you into all the truth**. He will not speak on his own; he will speak only what he hears, and he will tell you what is yet to come."* (John 16:13)

How can I know **what God's will is**?

*"Do not conform to the pattern of this world, but be transformed by the renewing of your mind. Then you will be able to test and approve **what God's will is**—his good, pleasing and perfect will."* (Romans 12:2)

How can I **plan my course** correctly to make the right decisions? Who **establishes my steps**?

*"In their hearts humans **plan their course**, but the* LORD ***establishes their steps**."* (Proverbs 16:9)

What if I **lack wisdom** about making a decision?

*"If any of you **lacks wisdom**, you should ask God, who gives generously to all without finding fault, and it will be given to you."* (James 1:5)

What can I do if I really want to **glorify God**?

*" ... whether you eat or drink or whatever you do, do it all for the **glory of God**."* (1 Corinthians 10:31)

What makes me **desire to do God's will**?

*"**I desire to do your will**, my God; your law is within my heart."* (Psalm 40:8)

NOTES

1. James Strong, *Strong's Hebrew Lexicon* (electronic edition; Online Bible Millennium Edition v. 1.13) (Timnathserah Inc., July 6, 2002).

2. James Strong, *Strong's Greek Lexicon* (electronic edition; Online Bible Millennium Edition v. 1.13) (Timnathserah Inc., July 6, 2002).

3. Strong, *Strong's Greek Lexicon*; W. E. Vine, *Vine's Complete Expository Dictionary of Biblical Words*, electronic ed. (Nashville: Thomas Nelson, 1996).

4. *Merriam-Webster Collegiate Dictionary* (2001); http://www.m-w.com.

5. Strong, *Strong's Greek Lexicon*; Vine, *Vine's Complete Expository Dictionary*.

6. *Merriam-Webster's Collegiate Dictionary*, s.v. "Discernment," http://www.m-w.com/cgi-bin/dictionary?book=Dictionary&va=discernment.

7. Lawrence J. Crabb, Jr., *Understanding People: Deep Longings for Relationship*, Ministry Resources Library (Grand Rapids: Zondervan, 1987), 15–16; Robert S. McGee, *The Search for Significance*, 2nd ed. (Houston, TX: Rapha, 1990), 27–30.

8. Discipleship Counseling Services, *Discipleship Counseling Training Student Manual* (Dallas: Discipleship Counseling Services, n.d.), n.p.

SELECTED BIBLIOGRAPHY

Blackaby, Henry T., and Claude V. King. *Experiencing God: How to Live in the Full Adventure of Knowing and Doing the Will of God.* Nashville: Broadman & Holman, 1994.

Discipleship Counseling Services. *Discipleship Counseling Training Student Manual.* Dallas: Discipleship Counseling Services, n.d.

Hunt, June. *Healing the Hurting Heart: Answers to Real Letters from Real People.* Dallas: Hope For The Heart, 1995.

Myers, Warren, and Ruth Myers. *Discovering God's Will: Experience Afresh How Good God Is.* Colorado Springs, CO: NavPress, 2000.

Packer, J. I., Dale Larson, and Sandy Larson. *Decisions: Finding God's Will: 6 Studies for Individuals or Groups.* Downers Grove, IL: InterVarsity, 1996.

Robinson, Haddon. *Decision-Making by the Book.* Wheaton, IL: Victor, 1991.

Smith, M. Blaine. *Knowing God's Will: Finding Guidance for Personal Decisions.* Rev. and expanded ed. Downers Grove, IL: InterVarsity, 1991.

Stanley, Charles F. *Walking Wisely: Real Guidance for Life's Journey.* Nashville: Oliver-Nelson, 2002.

Sweeting, George. *How to Discover the Will of God.* Chicago: Moody, 1975.

Swindoll, Charles R. *The Mystery of God's Will: What Does He Want for Me?* Nashville: W Publishing Group, 1999.

Waltke, Bruce. *Finding the Will of God: A Pagan Notion?* Gresham, OR: Vision House, 1995.

June Hunt's HOPE FOR THE HEART booklets are biblically-based, and full of practical advice that is relevant, spiritually-fulfilling and wholesome. Each topic presents scriptural truths and examples of real-life situations to help readers relate and integrate June's counseling guidance into their own lives. Practical for individuals from all walks of life, this new booklet series invites readers into invaluable restoration, emotional health, and spiritual freedom.

HOPE FOR THE HEART TITLES

www.aspirepress.com